Ancient China

The Nature Company Discoveries Library published by Time-Life Books

Conceived and produced by
Weldon Owen Pty Limited
43 Victoria Street, McMahons Point,
NSW, 2060, Australia
A member of the
Weldon Owen Group of Companies
Sydney • San Francisco
Copyright © 1996 US Weldon Owen Inc.
Copyright © 1996 Weldon Owen Pty Limited
Reprinted 1997

THE NATURE COMPANY
Priscilla Wrubel, Ed Strobin, Steve Manning,
Georganne Papac, Tracy Fortini

TIME-LIFE BOOKS
Time-Life Books is a division of Time Life Inc.
Time-Life is a trademark of Time Warner Inc.
U.S.A.

Time-Life Custom Publishing
Vice President and Publisher: Terry Newell
Director of New Product Development:
Quentin McAndrew
Managing Editor: Donia Ann Steele
Director of Sales: Neil Levin
Director of Financial Operations: J. Brian Birky

WELDON OWEN Pty Limited
Chairman: Kevin Weldon
President: John Owen
Publisher: Sheena Coupe
Managing Editor: Rosemary McDonald
Project Editor: Ann B. Bingaman
Text Editor: Claire Craig
Art Director: Sue Burk
Designers: Kathy Gammon, Jill Ryan
Visual Research Coordinator: Jenny Mills
Visual Research: Amanda Weir
Production Manager: Caroline Webber
Production Assistant: Kylie Lawson

Vice President, International Sales:
Stuart Laurence

Coeditions Director: Derek Barton

Text: Judith Simpson

Illustrators: Paul Bachem; Andrew Beckett/Garden
Studio; Leslye Cole/Alex Lavroff & Associates;
Chris Forsey; John Crawford Fraser; Lorraine
Hannay; Richard Hook/Bernard Thornton Artists,
UK; Janet Jones/Alex Lavroff & Associates;
Shane Marsh/Linden Artists; Iain McKellar;
Peter Mennim; Darren Pattenden/Garden Studio;
Tony Pyrzakowski; John Richards; Trevor Ruth;
Mark Sofilas/Alex Lavroff & Associates;
Sharif Tarabay/Garden Studio; CW Taylor;
Rod Westblade

Library of Congress
Cataloging-in-Publication Data
Ancient China / Judith Simpson.

    p. cm -- (Discoveries Library)

  Includes index.
  ISBN 0-8094-9248-2
  1. China--Civilization--Juvenile literature.
  [1. China--Civilization.] I. Title. II. Series.

  DS721.S56 1996

  931--dc20   95-31546

Manufactured by Mandarin Offset
Printed in China

A Weldon Owen Production

THE NATURE COMPANY
DISCOVERIES
LIBRARY

Ancient
China

CONSULTING EDITOR

Carol Michaelson
Assistant Keeper, Department of Oriental Antiquities
The British Museum, London

TIME
LIFE
BOOKS

Contents

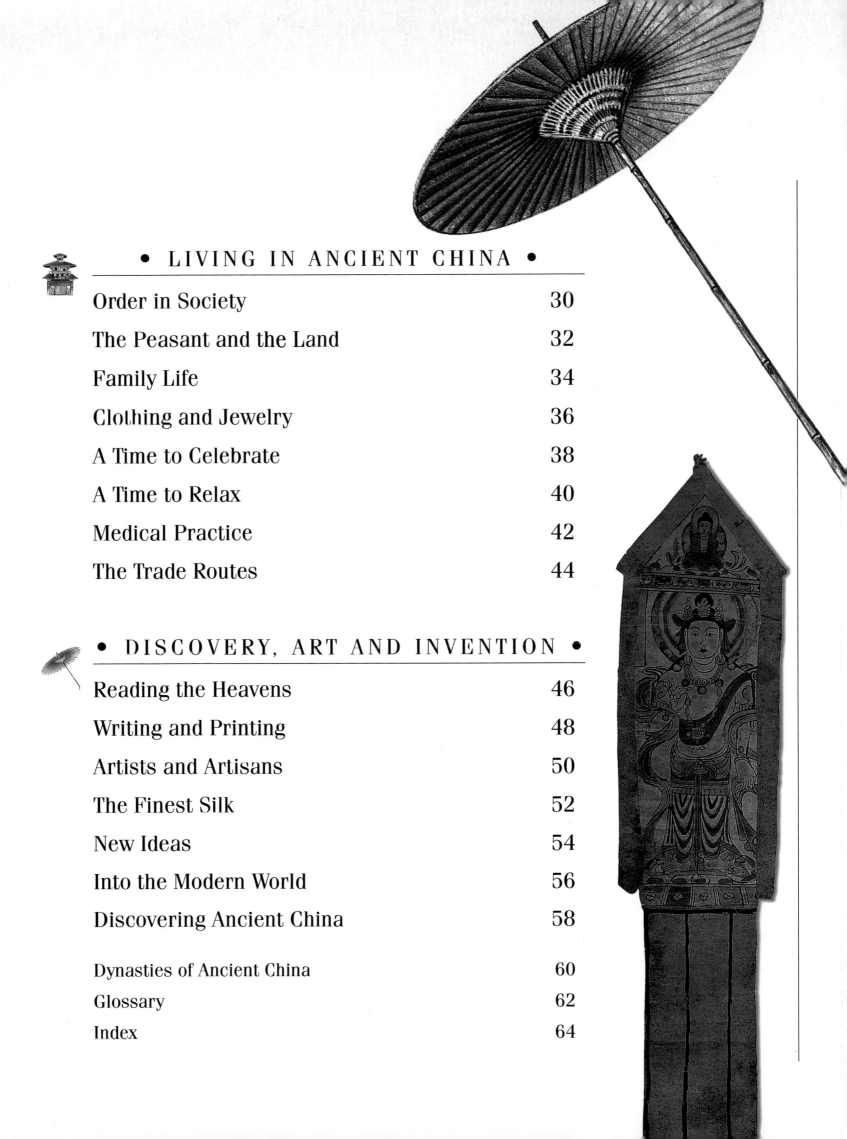

The Middle Kingdom

The civilization of ancient China began about 8,000 years ago, when people settled in areas of the northeast and beside three great rivers—the Yellow River in the north, the Wei River in the northwest and the Yangzi River in the south. They worked the soil with wood and stone tools, grew millet and rice, and raised pigs and dogs. For centuries, the ancient Chinese were enclosed by mountains, deserts and sea, and had little contact with the rest of the world. They developed their own way of life, and called their country "The Middle Kingdom" because they thought it was the center of the universe. Some Chinese leaders were buried in huge underground tombs. Soldiers, convicts and laborers built a wall to keep out northern invaders, and traders from the west traveled to China along the Silk Road.

TAKLAMAKAN DESERT

Wei River

HIMALAYAN MOUNTAINS

N

S

6

MONGOLIA

•Beijing

Yellow
River

Anyang
•

Grand Canal

•Zhengzhou

•Luoyang

anyang

•Xi'an
•Banpo
Chang'an

Yangzi River

6000–1700 BC
Stone Age
(Neolithic) period

Stone Age (Neolithic)
pot lid in the form of
a clay mask

2000–1600 BC
Erlitou period

1600–1050 BC
Shang dynasty

1050–221 BC
Zhou dynasty

Zhou bronze

221–207 BC
Qin dynasty

206 BC–AD 220
Han dynasty

AD 221–280
Three Kingdoms

AD 265–420
Jin dynasty

Han lacquerware

AD 386–581
Northern dynasties

AD 420–589
Southern dynasties

AD 581–618
Sui dynasty

AD 618–906
Tang dynasty

Tang terra cotta

Discover more in The Trade Routes

The Shang Dynasty

I n the Stone Age (Neolithic period), different groups lived in separate communities across the vast land of China. The first dynasty or line of rulers we know about was called the Shang. According to legend, there was a Xia dynasty before them but archaeologists have not yet found any written records from this era. Many things, however, including writing on bronze vessels and oracle bones, survive from Shang times. States fought each other for land until the Shang kings gained control in northern China and set up large cities. Peasants grew food for everyone and craftspeople made tools, weapons, clothing, ornaments and household goods from bronze, silk, jade, clay and other materials. The royal family lived inside a walled palace with their advisers, and diviners who predicted the future. When a king died, servants and animals were sacrificed to go with him to Heaven.

AN AGE OF BRONZE
The large number of containers and other objects made from bronze that survive from the Shang period show advanced methods of production. Artisans adapted ways of working in clay to working in metal. Molten bronze was poured into carved ceramic molds. When the metal cooled, the bronzesmith broke the mold, removed the clay core, and polished the metal surface.

WINE CONTAINER
The Shang liked to drink warm wine. This bronze vessel, made by the clay mold method of casting, was used to hold wine.

READING THE ORACLE BONES

The Shang believed that spirits of dead ancestors "spoke" to the living through oracle bones. These were the polished shoulder bones of oxen and sheep or the undershells of turtles. A diviner scraped furrows in an oracle bone and inscribed a question on it such as "Is it safe to go on a journey?" Then he scorched the bone and read the cracks that resulted from the heat as the answer to the question.

BURIED BRONZE
China's soil continues to reveal secrets about ancient times. In 1986, brickworkers accidentally uncovered this statue, taller than any man, and life-size heads with strange features.

Discover more in Artists and Artisans

LINKED DISKS
The belts and pendants of the wealthy were decorated with jade. This complicated piece is cleverly made from a single jade pebble.

• ANCIENT BEGINNINGS •

The Zhou Dynasty

Warlike Zhou people from the Wei River Valley in the northwest conquered the Shang and began a dynasty that lasted for more than 800 years. Zhou rulers enlarged the Shang kingdom and gave land to their relatives and advisers. At first, these noblemen were loyal to the Zhou kings. But during the Spring and Autumn periods and in the time of the Warring States, the local lords raised armies, forcing many peasants to become foot soldiers, and competed with one another for power. The Zhou era brought important changes. Cities grew in size and number, and merchants began to carry trade goods between them. Metalworkers forged iron tools and weapons. The use of iron plows made farming easier and increased food production. Scholars reacted to the unsettled times by thinking of ways to make ancient China a more peaceful country.

JADE DISK
Jade, more precious than gold in ancient China, was found in river beds and on mountain peaks. Jade was hard to carve, and elaborate objects sometimes took years to make.

MILITARY PROGRESS
New fighting methods were introduced du[r]ing the long clashes in the Warring States peri[od]. Mounted warriors, armed with bows and arrows, replaced the old-fashioned chariots. Low-born foot soldiers could now rise in rank to become officers in the army.

SCHOOLS OF THOUGHT

Many scholars who lived in Zhou times thought about law and order. Their ideas shaped society in the centuries to come. Three systems emerged most strongly. Confucianism taught obedience within the family and respect for ancestors. The followers of Daoism wanted as few rules as possible. A third school of thought, called Legalism, said that everyone must obey the state's ruler and contribute to the army and food production.

BURIED FOR CENTURIES

Unusual tomb goods survive from Zhou times. This bird may have guarded against evil spirits or been used to carry a musical instrument. Words on its beak say "For Zeng Hou Yi's eternal use."

Bronze bird with antlers

Bronze ritual vessel

THE ART OF INLAY

Zhou metalworkers began to inlay the surfaces of bronze vessels, weapons and chariot parts with silver and semi-precious stones or glass.

Discover more in Three Ways of Thinking

15

The Qin Dynasty

Qin Shi Huangdi

The powerful Qin conquered the six major kingdoms that remained at the end of the Warring States period. The king thanked his ancestors for his success and decided to drop the title wang, which meant "king." He renamed himself Shi (meaning "first" Huangdi (meaning "emperor and divine ruler"). The First Emperor was very important because he unified ancient China by making strict laws, taxing everyone in the country and introducing one script for writing. He commanded his subjects to build roads and canals, and to join existing walls into one long defensive wall. Qin Shi Huangdi did not agree with the teachings of Confucius and other scholars, and ordered their books to be burned. The First Emperor paid magicians, called alchemists, for potions to help him live forever. After his death, his dynasty soon collapsed.

STANDARD COINAGE
Early bronze coins were cast in some unusual shapes. The First Emperor introduced a standard system of money throughout China.

STANDARD WEIGHTS
Qin Shi Huangdi also standardized weights and measures. These included the bronze and terra-cotta cups used for measuring liquids and grains, and the bronze and iron weights that balanced scales.

DID YOU KNOW?
Qin Shi Huangdi, who wanted to live forever, has survived in one way. Qin, pronounced to sound like "chin," gave us the word "China." In a way, the First Emperor's name will never die.

TIGER IN TWO PIECES
An army commander had one part of this model tiger. Messages from the emperor arrived in the second piece to prove that the battle orders were not forged.

PROTECTING THE EMPEROR
In March 1974, well-diggers discovered a silent army guarding the tomb of Qin Shi Huangdi. Pit One contained more than 3,000 life-size foot soldiers and teams of chariot horses.

16

THE TERRA-COTTA WARRIORS

Qin Shi Huangdi's military companions for eternity march in three pits to the east of his tomb. A fourth pit is empty—the work unfinished at the end of the dynasty in 207 BC. The heads and bodies of the foot soldiers, charioteers and archers (like this one) were made in molds, but no two faces are the same. Some are bearded, others are clean-shaven. Eyes, noses, lips and ears are in many different shapes.

The Han Dynasty

Liu Bang, a government official, gained power and founded the Han dynasty, which lasted for more than 400 years. Han emperors strengthened the Qin system of government and extended ancient China's boundaries. They developed a civil service, based on the teachings of Confucius, to run the empire and keep records in a central place. Scholars who wanted to become government officials had to study very hard. The government organized the salt and iron mines, and state factories began mass-producing objects—from iron and steel farming tools to silk cloth and paper. Han emperors began to control the eastern end of the Silk Road that linked Asia and Europe. Buddhism, one of the most important foreign influences, started to spread throughout ancient China. The Han dynasty finally collapsed after a succession of weak child emperors and droughts and floods.

GILDED BRONZE LEOPARDS
These graceful animals with garnet eyes and inlaid silver spots came from Princess Dou Wan's tomb. They were used as weights.

WATER HIGHWAYS
During the Han era, the people were ordered to build canals to link the cities. These inland waterways made trading, collecting taxes and distributing food during famines much easier. Some families lived on houseboats. Babies often had bamboo floats tied to them until they learned to swim.

AMUSEMENTS FOR THE AFTERLIFE

Acrobats were popular entertainers in ancient China. This tray of tumbling pottery figures was made to amuse the dead in the afterlife.

GOVERNMENT TRANSPORT

Important government officials traveled by horse and carriage. Small models of these were made for their tombs so they would not have to walk in the afterlife.

THE GRAND CANAL

In the Sui period, Emperor Yang decided to link the Yangzi and Yellow rivers by joining new and existing canals. This waterway of 1,550 miles (2,500 km) carried grain and soldiers across his empire. The Grand Canal took more than 30 years to build, and all men 15–50 years of age worked on the project. Every family living nearby also had to send an old man, a woman and a child to the labor force.

Beijing

Grand Canal

Shanghai

China

Q: Why did the Han dynasty collapse?

THE IMPORTANCE OF HORSES
Horses were a sign of great wealth in ancient China. Lifelike pottery models were often buried in the tombs of noblemen.

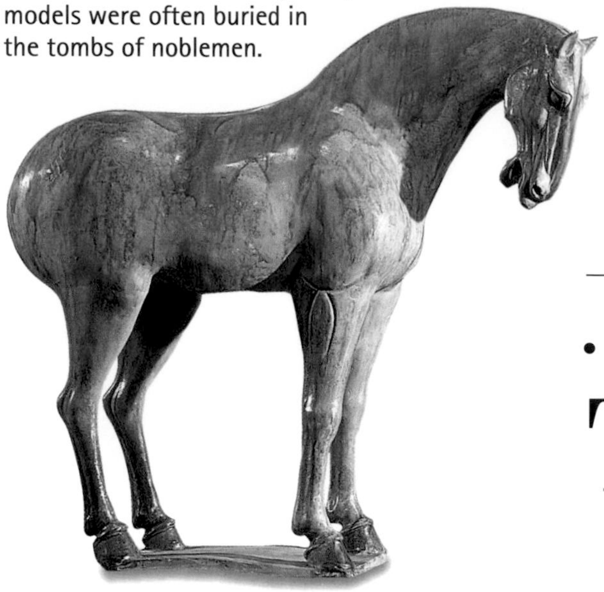

CITY MARKETS
Chang'an was the capital of the Han, Sui and Tang empires. By the Tang era, the busy western market was crammed with warehouses. Foreign merchants brought goods from central and western Asia, India and beyond.

• ANCIENT BEGINNINGS •

The Tang Dynasty

The Tang dynasty ruled ancient China for 300 years. This was a time when art, craft, music and literature further developed, and people called it a golden age. Boundaries expanded again as Tang armies fought successfully against the Koreans in the north, the Vietnamese in the south, and the Tibetans and Turks in the west. The Chinese traded with people from these lands and learned much more about the world beyond China. Buddhism, Confucianism and Daoism were still very important, but traders brought other religious ideas to China along the Silk Road. Visiting craftspeople to the city of Chang'an taught local artisans different ways of making things. Clothing showed the influence of foreign fashions. The wealthy developed a taste for imported foods. They ate dumplings in 24 flavors, tasty sauces, and ice cream made from chilled milk, rice and camphor. Tea, made from the leaves of bushes grown in the warm south, reached northern China's markets during the Tang period, and rich people also enjoyed this new drink.

PATTERNS FROM PERSIA
Chinese artisans copied traditional Persian decoration. The mounted hunter on the side of this jug is copied from a Persian design.

SKILLED ARTISTS
This is part of a painting on silk called *The Eight Noble Officials.* The figures in their flowing garments show the lively style used by Tang artists.

DID YOU KNOW?

Chang'an was laid out in a square. The four walls had three gates in each wall. Each gate had three gateways—the emperor alone used the central one.

FOREIGN WAYS

During the Tang period, gold and silver became more highly prized than before, and rivaled jade and bronze in value. Persian metalworkers, who fled from their own country and came to live in Chang'an, taught the Chinese more delicate methods of using these precious metals. Tang jewelers began to beat them into thin sheets and to make objects from threads of metal.

STROLLING PLAYERS

Goods for sale were loaded onto the backs of camels and into wagons pulled by oxen. Foreign traders, Chinese merchants and the local crowd enjoyed performances by street acrobats and storytellers.

FOREIGN TONGUES

Among the noisy chatter in the market place, the people of Chang'an heard travelers speaking languages from other parts of the world.

ANCIENT DRAGON

Animal charms were supposed to protect their owners against evil influences. This jade dragon was modeled during the Shang period.

PAN GU'S WORLD

The mythical Pan Gu turned his watery world into stone and then shaped the moon, sun and stars, and floated them in space. He asked the phoenix (also known as the vermilion bird), the Chinese unicorn (or qilin), the dragon and the tortoise to help him.

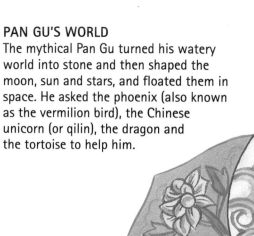

• HEAVEN AND EARTH •

Myths and Symbols

Ancient Chinese myths explain the world's beginning. One story tells of Pan Gu whose body parts became nature after he died. His breath, for example, changed into the wind and clouds, his hair and beard into stars. In another legend, the goddess Nu Gua modeled some human figures from mud. They became rich nobles. Growing tired of such hard work, Nu Gua scattered drops of mud to form poor people. Real and imaginary animals were also featured in ancient Chinese folklore. The blue dragon was linked with spring, the east and rain; the red phoenix bird with summer, the south and drought. The white tiger of the west represented autumn, strength and courage. The black tortoise was associated with winter, the north, long life and wisdom. It was also said that animals were invited to a banquet in Heaven, in which 12—the rat, ox, tiger, rabbit, dragon, snake, horse, goat, monkey, rooster, dog and boar—were chosen to represent the 12-year cycle. Chinese people still link these animals with the year of their birth.

CARRIER BIRD

Mythical animals were often modeled in bronze. This bird, studded with turquoise, has a jade bi disk in its beak. The side cups may have held cosmetics.

YIN AND YANG

Before the world began, there was chaos, shaped like a hen's egg. Pan Gu separated this egg into Yin and Yang—two parts of the same whole. Yin formed the heavier Earth; Yang formed the lighter sky. From then on, Yin stood for all the female, wet, dark things of nature; while Yang represented everything that was male, dry and bright. There could be no perfect happiness until there was an equal balance between Yin and Yang.

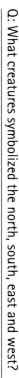

GATHERERS OF CLOUDS
Dragons were the rain spirits of ancient China. A Tang jeweler crafted this golden beast with claws outstretched.

MURAL FROM THE HAN ERA
Tigers were popular in Chinese mythology. They were painted on the walls of houses to ward off harm.

DID YOU KNOW?
In ancient Chinese art, horses were symbols of speed and high rank, water buffalo stood for the peasant's life of toil, and flying birds represented freedom.

Discover more in A Time to Celebrate

23

As jade seemed to last forever, the ancient Chinese believed this "stone of Heaven" prevented the body from decaying after death. In the Han dynasty, some royal persons were buried in suits made from tiny pieces of jade.

• HEAVEN AND EARTH •

Sons of Heaven

People believed that kings or emperors received heavenly approval to rule. This was called the mandate of Heaven. The mandate was the idea that the country's leader was the Son of Heaven and obtained power from his celestial or heavenly forefathers. Rulers took part in special ceremonies to ask their ancestors to make sure that rain fell at the right time, that it was safe to go on a journey, that hunting was successful and that many other daily events turned out well. An emperor's subjects expected him to be wise, hard-working, unselfish, good and a brilliant military leader. People rebelled against a bad or weak ruler who did not care about their wellbeing, and believed the heavenly spirits showed their displeasure with him through earthquakes, droughts, famine or floods. The mandate was then taken away and given to someone else.

SYMBOLS OF POWER
A number of jade blades have been discovered from Shang times. They were possibly used during ritual ceremonies and perhaps showed the owner's rank or position in society.

"DAUGHTER" OF HEAVEN

The phoenix bird symbolized an empress. Wu Zetian came to power after the death of her husband Gaozong, a weak emperor during the Tang dynasty. Although other women ruled ancient China at various times, Empress Wu Zetian was the only one to claim she had the mandate of Heaven. She chose her advisers from officials who had passed exams instead of favoring people from rich families.

THE EMPEROR'S COURT
In the Tang dynasty, Sons of Heaven ruled the greatest empire in the whole of the ancient world. They displayed their outstanding wealth at court. Gold glittered and silk shone when the emperors exchanged gifts with ambassadors from foreign lands.

COFFIN COVERING
Coffins often nested one inside the other. Sometimes a silk cloak covered the innermost one—perhaps to clothe the dead person on his or her flight to Heaven.

RIDING IN STATE
A model state coach found near the First Emperor's tomb was drawn by four horses harnessed in gold. It had gold furnishings, and doors and windows that opened.

• HEAVEN AND EARTH •

In Life and Death

The ancient Chinese worshipped their ancestors and looked to them for advice on how to manage their daily lives. The ruler spent many hours communicating with his royal forefathers during special ceremonies. They "spoke" to him through oracle bones and other rituals, and advised him on how to run the country. People believed that life continued after death and that they would need their worldly goods when they joined their ancestors in Heaven. The poor went to their graves in cheap coffins with very few possessions. At first, the tombs of the rich contained human sacrifices. In later times, artisans began making copies of servants and attendants in clay, wood or bronze. Burial pits contained many chambers with walls and ceilings decorated to look like the rooms of real houses. Soldiers and mythological creatures guarded the entrance tunnels.

TANG TOMB GUARD
This glazed pottery official shared his duties as a tomb guard with another official, two spirits, two Buddhist guards, two horses, two camels and three grooms.

FIT FOR A PRINCESS
Princess Yongtai died during the Tang dynasty. Her tomb furnishings reflected her high position in life. Some of the walls were covered with exquisite drawings. Jars of wine, food and other household goods made sure she would want for nothing.

A TUNEFUL AFTERLIFE

Musicians often played bells for ancient Chinese lords at solemn rituals or to entertain visitors. This perfectly preserved set of 64 bronze bells mounted on a wooden rack was found in a Zhou tomb. When struck with a wooden stick, each bell produced two notes. The bells in the second row chimed the melody; the larger ones at the bottom provided the accompaniment.

Discover more in The Shang Dynasty

Three Ways of Thinking

Three ways of thinking—Confucianism, Daoism and Buddhism—influenced the ancient Chinese. Each one might help with a different part of life. Confucius outlined a code of proper behavior, arguing that if families were strong and united, the country would also be strong and united. He praised strict government. The followers of Daoism did not agree. They said that everyone should live by the laws of nature and should not be governed by too many regulations made by people. Daoists thought that there would be fewer wars and crimes when people stopped wanting things they could not obtain honestly. Buddhism taught believers that they could be reincarnated (born again) many times, and that performing good deeds in this life meant better chances in the next one. Besides these ways of thinking, foreigners brought Christianity, Judaism and the beliefs of Islam into ancient China.

DID YOU KNOW?

Daoists worshipped a small group of "immortals," or disciples, who were supposed to possess magical powers such as becoming invisible, turning objects into gold and raising the dead.

TEMPLE STATUES
Some Buddhist statues in the cave temples were made from a clay mixture called stucco, which lasted well. However, the surface painting was often damaged.

ACCORDING TO THE MASTER

Ren, represented by this Chinese written character, was the basis of Confucian teaching. Ren is often translated as virtue or goodness. Confucius himself explained ren as "to love all men." The sayings of Confucius were collected in a book called *The Analects*. The Master said that society would be orderly if prince, subject, father and son kept to their proper places.

CAVES OF A THOUSAND BUDDHAS

Buddhist monks hollowed temples out of caves in remote places. They decorated the walls with detailed images of Buddha and his disciples. Some caves contained portraits painted on paper banners such as this one, or on silk cloth.

Discover more in Writing and Printing

Scholar

Peasant

Artisan

Merchant

Order in Society

Ancient Chinese society was divided into four main classes. The scholar–gentry class was the highest and most esteemed. Scholars were respected above everyone else because they could read and write. Peasants were the next most important class because the country depended on them to produce food. Artisans (people who worked with their hands) used their skills to make things that everyone needed, such as weapons, tools and cooking utensils. The lowest class were merchants. They made nothing, yet often grew rich from trading goods. Laws governed the lifestyle of people in all classes. The size and decoration of officials' houses depended on their rank. An official of the third rank could build a house with five pillars in a row. Officials of the highest importance could add a gate that was three pillars wide.

A MAGISTRATE'S DUTIES

A district magistrate was a low ranking official in the many-layered government bureaucracy, or organization. He enforced law and order; collected taxes; counted people; registered births, deaths, marriages and property; inspected schools; supervised building programs; and judged court cases.

IN ORDER OF IMPORTANCE

Scholars, peasants, artisans and merchants formed the basic social order of ancient China. Soldiers who made a career of being in the army were not highly regarded and did not belong to a class of their own.

BECOMING A PUBLIC SERVANT

Scholars who were interested in the government trained for the imperial civil service. Han Emperor Wu started a university where students learned the teachings of Confucius. These men usually came from wealthy land-owning families, but anyone could take the imperial civil service exams, and sometimes whole villages sponsored a candidate. The few who passed the exams became government officials and magistrates.

A VERDICT OF GUILTY
When the court believed that evidence collected by investigators or statements from witnesses were enough to prove a person's guilt, the accused was encouraged to confess.

DID YOU KNOW?
Government officials, called censors, had the task of investigating cases of injustice or poor government. They also informed the emperor if they thought he was failing in his duties.

Discover more in The Han Dynasty

NEW WAYS OF FARMING
In the Zhou dynasty, farmers began to use oxen to draw their iron plows. The crop carved along the top of this Han dynasty gravestone is millet.

MODEL GRANARY
Harvested grain was stored in a granary, the most important building on an ancient Chinese farm. This knee-high tomb model of a granary is made from glazed terra cotta.

EARLY HOEING
This stone carving shows the mythical father of Chinese agriculture, Shen Nong, digging with a two-pronged stick.

• LIVING IN ANCIENT CHINA •

The Peasant and the Land

Peasant farmers cultivated small plots, and supplied food to the army and to people in the cities. Farmers made the most of the space by cutting terraces into the hill slopes. In spring, there was an important ceremony when the emperor went to the fields to plow the first furrow. Farmers in the north grew barley, wheat and millet to eat, and hemp for clothing. Those in the south planted rice in the soft mud of the flooded paddy fields. Vegetables, such as snow-peas, and lychees and other fruits supplemented these main crops. In some regions, the women raised silkworms. Every able-bodied person in a farming family worked from dawn to dusk. "Agriculture is the foundation of the world," said Han Emperor Wu, but peasants also had to serve in the army and help with government projects such as building walls, canals and dykes.

DEEP FURROWS
Farmers plowed after rain. Hard iron plows, which turned damp soil more easily, replaced softer ones made from wood or bronze. Peasants kept few large animals because they did not want to waste their precious land growing fodder for livestock.

PROBLEMS WITH WATER

In some regions, peasants pedaled irrigation machines to raise water from canals and streams so that their growing crops had regular moisture. The Yellow River spread rich, fertile silt across the valley in good years. But sometimes this great waterway dried to a trickle. At other times, it flooded or changed its course and destroyed whole villages.

DID YOU KNOW?

Everyone had to pay taxes in ancient China. Farmers often paid their taxes in the form of grain or in time spent working for the government.

Discover more in Discovering Ancient China

Family Life

Generations of Chinese families lived together in the same house. Grandfathers, fathers and uncles were considered more important than grandmothers, mothers and aunts, and the birth of a boy was celebrated more than the birth of a girl. The first household rule was that sons and daughters should obey their parents at all times. Children were taught that they must care for their mothers and fathers in sickness and old age. Grandmothers became very important when their husbands died because old people were greatly respected. This was how many women from royal families obtained power in ancient China. When a girl married, she left home and had to obey her husband and parents-in-law. Poor families sometimes sold their daughters to be servants of the rich.

PAINTED JAR

From earliest times, the ancient Chinese shaped, decorated and fired clay objects. This lidded earthenware vessel was made by a Han potter.

DID YOU KNOW?

Ancient Chinese names reflected the importance of the family. The family name was always written or spoken first and the personal name came last. This is still the custom today.

LACQUERED TABLEWARE

Wealthy people used lacquered wooden tableware. Gold, silver and jade banquet vessels were introduced during the Tang dynasty.

FAMILY GATHERINGS

During festivals, a more relaxed atmosphere replaced the strict daily routines of home. Families might go together to visit the graves of ancestors and fathers would spend time with their wives and children.

MINIATURE MANSIONS
Clay models from Han tombs tell us that the well-to-do lived in large houses built around spacious courtyards. These mansions had gatehouses and watch towers.

ANCESTOR WORSHIP

Long before Confucius drew up his code of behavior and encouraged ancestor worship, the ancient Chinese believed that the living could "talk" to their forefathers in Heaven. In most family homes, there was an altar for making offerings to the dead, and bronze ritual food vessels were often engraved with family achievements and honors.
In return for this respect, people expected the spirits to protect and look after them.

35

Emperor's hat (mian)

Lacquered gauze cage hat

Water chestnut kerchief hat

Warrior's helmet

Gauze turban (fu tou)

PROPER HEADGEAR
A man's hat completed his outfit, and he would not be seen in public without one. Hat fashions changed through the ages, but they always showed the wearer's occupation and status.

DECORATIVE COMB
Women's long hair was arranged in topknots, held in place by hairpins and other ornaments. The pattern on this comb was hammered out by a jeweler.

Clothing and Jewelry

Clothing was a mark of class in ancient China. Fabric textures, colors and decoration, jewelry, headgear and footwear all told something about the wearer's rank and position in society. High-ranking officials dressed in the finest silk for public outings and celebrations, and in less expensive clothes at home. Peasants wore a long, shirtlike garment, made of undyed hemp fiber, which altered little until modern times. During some dynasties, the scholar–gentry class wore jade, gold, silver and brass jewelry, while everyone else had copper and iron accessories. Fashions for the wealthy changed as the years passed. Tang noblewomen, for example, favored the hundred-bird feather skirt, but this was later banned to prevent rare birds from becoming extinct. Tang poems praised women's elaborate make-up. One poem claimed that layers of carefully applied face powder and rouge created "a vision of loveliness."

UPTURNED TOES
Some silk brocade shoes, made for the nobility, have survived in the tombs. This fashionable pair belonged to Lady Xin, Marquise of Dai.

TANG FASHION
The scholar–gentry class dressed in flowing, silk clothes. Fashionable women wore a long skirt and jacket, topped by a short-sleeved upper garment.

ZHOU BEADS

The craftspeople who made these beads copied designs from Egypt and the Middle East. Layers of colored glass formed a decoration known as the eyes.

TANG FASHION

Men wore loose robes. The wide sleeves were weighted so they hung down without flapping.

THE MAGIC OF MIRRORS

From Han times, polished bronze mirrors were mass-produced. Their beautifully patterned backs represented harmony within the universe. Smaller mirrors, thought to ward off evil spirits, hung from cords at the waist.

FOLLOWERS OF FASHION

Tang princesses wore the latest styles in gowns, shoes and hairdressing. Some design ideas, like the flowers on this dress material, came from countries outside China.

THE IMPORTANCE OF COLOR

Cloth in ancient China was colored with vegetable dyes, and the color of clothing indicated importance. This color coding changed as one dynasty succeeded another. From Sui times onward, only emperors were allowed to wear yellow. Ordinary people had to dress in blue and black. In AD 674, the government made stricter laws to stop people from hiding colored clothing underneath their outer garments. White was for mourning, and children could not wear white while their parents were alive.

37

A Time to Celebrate

Festival days provided a rest from hard daily work. The Spring Festival, which welcomed the new year, lasted for several days. People lit lanterns and exploded bamboo firecrackers. They ate specially prepared vegetable dishes, drank spiced wine, watched street entertainment, and took part in ceremonies to cast out demons. Many festivals dated from Han and Tang times, but Cold Food Day reminded people of Jie Zhi Tui, who served Prince Chong Er loyally during the Spring and Autumn period. When Jie Zhi Tui died in a fire, Chong Er declared an annual festival in his memory. On Cold Food Day, kitchen fires were put out and no cooking was done. Children in the emperor's palace competed to kindle new fire by twirling sticks on wooden boards for a prize of three rolls of silk cloth and a lacquered bowl. Some ancient festivals are still important in China today.

FOOD FOR A BANQUET
Food for noblemen's feasts was roasted, fried, steamed, stewed, sun-dried or pickled. Cooks seasoned some dishes with salt, and plum and soy sauces. They sweetened others with sugar and honey, or added ginger, garlic and cinnamon. The Chinese ate with chopsticks when most ancient people still used their fingers.

LAST DROPS
Ladles, shaped from lacquered wood, were used to scoop wine from deep storage jars. The ancient Chinese made wine from rice.

MUSICAL ACCOMPANIMENT
Musicians performed at banquets and solemn ceremonies. In this group, three players pluck zithers with 25 strings. The other two blow bamboo mouth organs.

TANG TABLEWARE
In Tang times, metalsmiths began to hammer out sheets of gold and silver to make cups and bowls. Banquet tables were set with beautifully shaped vessels decorated with graceful designs.

Dragon Boat Festival

The Dragon Boat Festival, held on the fifth day of the fifth month, is still celebrated today. Rowing boats, decorated at prow and stern to look like dragons, race on lakes and rivers as part of the celebrations. Other craft took to the water in ancient times. Paintings show people enjoying the day in pleasure boats with an upper and lower deck.

Discover more in In Life and Death

39

FLYING KITES
Kites, first made of silk and bamboo, became lighter and more elaborate once paper was invented. The Han army used them occasionally to frighten their enemies. Kites took prayers to Heaven and also provided hours of fun for both children and adults.

FOREVER DANCING
The standard of entertainment in Tang times was very high. Graceful figures of dancers, made from clay, were found in burial chambers at Chang'an.

STRUMMING THE STRINGS
Evidence from Tang paintings and tomb models suggests that noblewomen often performed at court. They sometimes played an instrument called the pipa, which looked like a lute.

A Time to Relax

The ancient Chinese loved entertainment. People attended theater and magic shows, acrobatics and martial arts displays, dancing, opera and musical performances. Among the instruments in the orchestra were metal and stone chimes, bamboo flutes and silk-stringed zithers. Confucius thought that harmonious sounds to soothe the soul were nearly as important as food for the body. Both men and women played games such as polo and a form of football, using a ball made from skin. Tang Emperor Xuanzong organized tug-of-war competitions on the festive Pure Brightness Day. An onlooker recorded that the noise of beating drums and cheering crowds was deafening. When spring warmed the air and peach trees blossomed, the ladies at court returned to the palace gardens to swing among the budding willows. They competed against one another to reach the dizziest heights.

40

THE NOBLE GAME OF POLO

Polo, played from horseback, became a favorite game at the Tang court. The invention of the stirrup gave competitors much better control of their horses. Matches were held in the palace grounds at Chang'an where Emperor Zhongzong's team of four players once beat a team of ten from Tibet. Emperor Xuanzong enjoyed polo so much that he neglected his imperial duties.

HOME ENTERTAINMENT
Noblemen invited acrobats, dancers, musicians and other entertainers into their homes to amuse their guests. Performances often lasted for hours.

DID YOU KNOW?
A special Music Bureau was set up during the Han dynasty. Its staff collected official and popular songs and musical compositions.

CAMEL TRANSPORT
Groups of professional musicians traveled from place to place to perform at banquets and ceremonies. Sometimes they traveled on camels, which could carry heavy loads.

Discover more in The Tang Dynasty

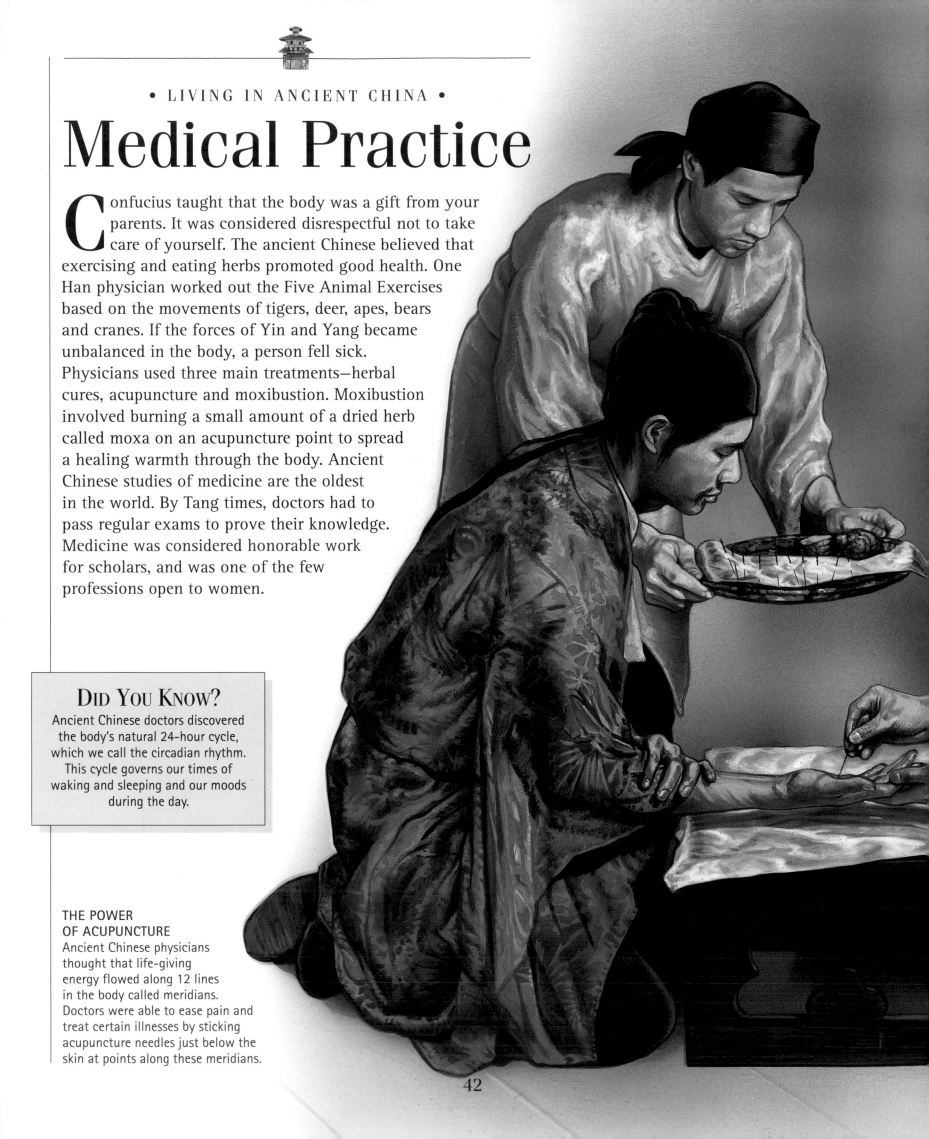

Medical Practice

Confucius taught that the body was a gift from your parents. It was considered disrespectful not to take care of yourself. The ancient Chinese believed that exercising and eating herbs promoted good health. One Han physician worked out the Five Animal Exercises based on the movements of tigers, deer, apes, bears and cranes. If the forces of Yin and Yang became unbalanced in the body, a person fell sick. Physicians used three main treatments—herbal cures, acupuncture and moxibustion. Moxibustion involved burning a small amount of a dried herb called moxa on an acupuncture point to spread a healing warmth through the body. Ancient Chinese studies of medicine are the oldest in the world. By Tang times, doctors had to pass regular exams to prove their knowledge. Medicine was considered honorable work for scholars, and was one of the few professions open to women.

DID YOU KNOW?

Ancient Chinese doctors discovered the body's natural 24-hour cycle, which we call the circadian rhythm. This cycle governs our times of waking and sleeping and our moods during the day.

THE POWER OF ACUPUNCTURE

Ancient Chinese physicians thought that life-giving energy flowed along 12 lines in the body called meridians. Doctors were able to ease pain and treat certain illnesses by sticking acupuncture needles just below the skin at points along these meridians.

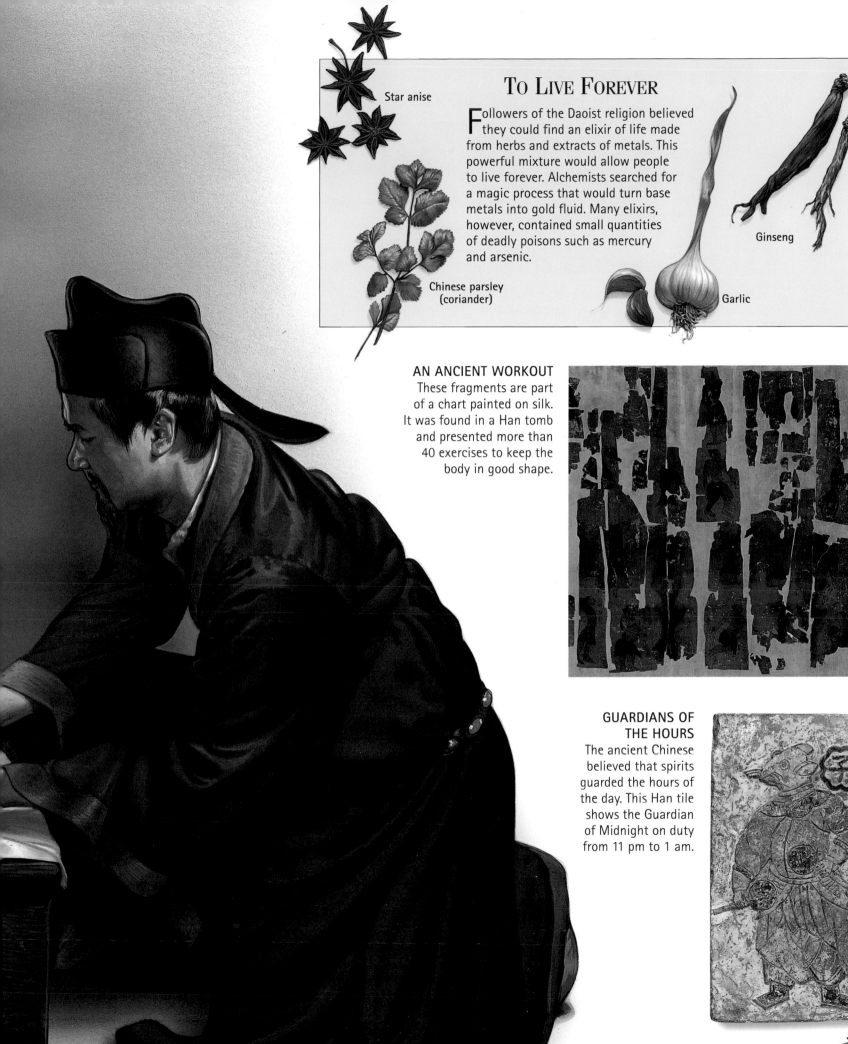

TO LIVE FOREVER

Followers of the Daoist religion believed they could find an elixir of life made from herbs and extracts of metals. This powerful mixture would allow people to live forever. Alchemists searched for a magic process that would turn base metals into gold fluid. Many elixirs, however, contained small quantities of deadly poisons such as mercury and arsenic.

Star anise

Chinese parsley (coriander)

Ginseng

Garlic

AN ANCIENT WORKOUT

These fragments are part of a chart painted on silk. It was found in a Han tomb and presented more than 40 exercises to keep the body in good shape.

GUARDIANS OF THE HOURS

The ancient Chinese believed that spirits guarded the hours of the day. This Han tile shows the Guardian of Midnight on duty from 11 pm to 1 am.

Discover more in Family Life

The Trade Routes

Trade began when neighboring peoples wanted luxury goods made in China. At first, there was more raiding than trading, but soon the Chinese began to exchange silk for the Ferghana horses of central Asia. Overland, the Silk Road eventually extended from Chang'an in China to the Mediterranean lands. This route was only possible because the ancient Chinese had camels for transport. These beasts each carried 440 lb (200 kg) of cargo around the "white dragon dunes" of the terrible Taklamakan Desert. They could smell underground water, and warned their riders of deadly, suffocating sandstorms by huddling together, snarling and burying their mouths in the sand.

From at least as early as Han times, sea routes took Chinese traders to Vietnam and later to Korea and Japan. Inside China, merchants transported goods such as grain and salt along the canals and roads that linked the large cities.

WESTERN WINE
This pottery figure of a westerner who lived in Chang'an's foreign community was found in a Tang tomb.

KASHGAR MARKETS
In Han times, Chinese camel caravans stopped at Kashgar in central Asia. From there, Middle Eastern merchants, who wanted a share of the profits, took the expensive goods to distant places such as ancient Rome, which bordered the Mediterranean Sea.

LIVES OF LUXURY
Trade goods made people's lives more comfortable. Merchants exchanged Chinese silk, lacquerware, tea and spices for gold, silver, glass, wool, pearls, furs and other luxuries.

VITAL FOR SURVIVAL
The Chinese needed horses to help fight off mounted nomads roaming their borders. Horses were difficult to breed in northern China so the Chinese imported them.

THE SILK ROAD
In 139 BC, Emperor Wu sent his minister Zhang Qian to Ferghana in central Asia to buy horses. On the way, he was captured by the Xiongnu. When Zhang Qian returned to China ten years later, he brought valuable information about countries to the west. The first Chinese merchants set out into central Asia in 114 BC. This trade route became known as the Silk Road. Within a few years camel caravans traveled frequently along it.

Q: Why was the camel a suitable beast in the desert?

Reading the Heavens

The ancient Chinese believed the night sky could tell them what was about to happen on Earth. Court astronomers studied the stars to improve their methods of making predictions to the emperor. People expected the Son of Heaven to reign in harmony with the universe, and to be able to foretell celestial events. His failure to do this might mean that he was unfit to rule. By 1300 BC, astronomers were recording eclipses of the sun and moon and movements of comets. Later, star catalogs listed individual stars with great precision. Writings on astronomy discovered in one Han tomb showed detailed knowledge of heavenly bodies such as the planets Venus, Jupiter, Mercury, Mars and Saturn. Only a select few were permitted to read the Heavens. There were severe punishments for ordinary people who tried to own astronomical instruments or chart the stars.

STUDYING THE STARS
Every night, astronomers went out to the city walls to observe and record the stars. They had maps of the sky and instruments to help them. Astronomers believed that the appearance of a comet indicated forthcoming disaster.

ASTRONOMICAL MAP
The ancient Chinese grouped the stars into 28 houses. On this box lid, the names of the houses circle the written symbol for the Great Bear star.

STARS IN STONE
This engraving shows five star groups and the animals or persons linked with them. The hare, at the top left, symbolizes the constellation Fang.

CHARTING THE STARS

The Chinese began reading the Heavens a long time ago. Eclipses of the sun and the moon are recorded on Shang oracle bones, and Shang astronomers marked the changing seasons by the stars. This ancient Chinese star chart was based on the work of three astronomers who lived in the fourth century BC. It was the custom to record groups of stars as circles linked with lines.

MEASURING THE STARS
The ancient Chinese used an armillary sphere to measure the stars. It is a collection of bronze rings, each marked as a gauge of measurement. The rings represent imaginary lines round the Earth, such as the equator.

Discover more in Myths and Symbols

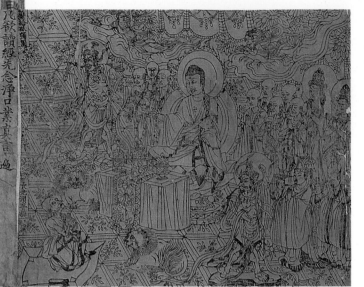

FIRST EDITION
Probably the earliest complete printed book to survive is a Buddhist text called *The Diamond Sutra*, printed in AD 868. It is in the form of a scroll nearly 20 ft (6 m) long.

SIGNED WITH A SEAL
Seals, usually impressed into red ink paste, frequently replaced signatures. The seals had from one to dozens of characters, and were carved or molded from bronze, silver, stone, horn, wood or jade.

DROP BY DROP
A calligrapher had special equipment, such as this pottery water dropper in the shape of a duck.

• DISCOVERY, ART AND INVENTION •

Writing and Printing

JADE BRUSH REST
Brush rests, often designed in animal forms, stopped wet brushes from rolling when the calligrapher was not using them.

Writing began to develop very early in ancient China. Early inscriptions were written on oracle bones and then on bronze ritual vessels. Bamboo strips, wooden tablets and pieces of silk were also used as writing materials. In about AD 105, government official Cai Lun suggested that pulping bark, roots, rags and old fishnets would improve the quality of paper, which had been invented several centuries before. This process was one of the most important discoveries of all time. In the Tang era, impressions from seals and the making of ink rubbings of engraved stone tablets led to the idea of printing. Text was written on fine paper and pasted, front side down, onto a wooden block. The printer cut away the background to leave raised characters. He then inked the surface of the block and pressed paper sheets against it to produce an image that was the right way up.

KEEPING THE RECORDS
Before people had paper, they wrote on bamboo, cutting the characters into the thin strips of wood from top to bottom. Many government records survive in this form.

CHINESE CHARACTERS

Chinese writing uses symbols for words and phrases and is read vertically (down and up) rather than horizontally (side to side). Some characters have up to 26 brushstrokes, which must be drawn in the correct order. Qin Shi Huangdi ordered a standard form of writing so that imperial commands could be read throughout the country. This script has not changed much until recent times.

口
mouth

日
sun

月
moon

王
ruler, king

THE ART OF CALLIGRAPHY
Ancient Chinese calligraphers wrote with brushes made from animal hairs, tied together with fine silk threads and glued in bamboo tubes. Calligraphers mixed their ink by rubbing a solid ink stick with drops of water on an ink stone.

Artists and Artisans

Painting was an important art form that developed alongside calligraphy. Artists had to perfect their brushstrokes, use a variety of colors, produce well-balanced compositions and represent their subject matter accurately. From the fourth century AD, painters were often recognized by name, but artisans who worked in teams usually remained anonymous. They made bronze, jade, clay and other materials into beautiful objects for religious rituals and household purposes, and fashioned thousands of tomb models of almost everything to do with daily life. Once the process of iron casting was developed, governments set up iron foundries to mass-produce agricultural tools and military weapons. Other state factories turned out lacquerware and silk cloth.

In the ninth century AD, an Arab author, Jahiz of Basra, commented that the Turks were the greatest soldiers, the Persians the best kings and the Chinese the most gifted of all craftspeople.

THE ART OF LACQUER
Sap from the lacquer tree is the oldest industrial plastic known to humans. Wood, bamboo or cloth utensils, coated with many thin layers of lacquer, can withstand the heat of cooking. The ancient Chinese colored lacquer black, red, brown, yellow, gold and green.

JADE DRAGON
The ancient Chinese valued jade, the "Stone of Heaven," above all other materials. Dragons, which were believed to have special powers, appeared frequently in their art.

TURNING THE PAGE
Books with bound pages took the place of scrolls in ancient China during the Tang dynasty. By this time, more women were learning to read.

WINE VESSEL
Birds with long plumes began appearing as decoration on bronze containers made in the middle Western Zhou period.

50

PATTERNED BOXES
Han potters were the first to glaze with lead. By the Tang period, lead-glazed ceramics were more boldly decorated. Potters often chose bright colors.

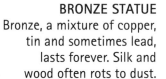

PEOPLE OF JADE
Hard jade stone was difficult to work. It was shaped with bamboo drills tipped with bronze, rubbed smooth with abrasive rock sand, and buffed on wood and leather polishing wheels.

BRONZE STATUE
Bronze, a mixture of copper, tin and sometimes lead, lasts forever. Silk and wood often rots to dust.

LACQUER ON THE LINE
Wealthy Chinese babies were fed using lacquer spoons and lacquer bowls. Wealthy Chinese people were buried in lacquer coffins. Artisans on production lines turned out many thousands of costly lacquer goods. This wine cup, surviving from the Han dynasty, is inscribed with the names of eight artisans and five supervisory officials who helped to produce the vessel.

Discover more in The Zhou Dynasty

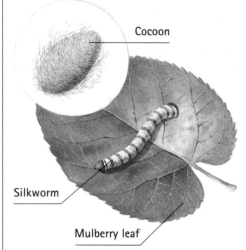

Cocoon

Silkworm

Mulberry leaf

LIFE CYCLE
Female silkworm moths lay hundreds of eggs. After hatching, the caterpillars eat steadily, shedding their tight skins four times as they grow. In four to five weeks they spin cocoons to protect them while they pupate into moths.

The Finest Silk

The filament from one silkworm's cocoon is several hundred feet long and it takes many thousands of filaments to produce enough thread for a dress length of fabric. The ancient Chinese wrote and painted on this expensive material, and made bed quilts and bags from it. Emperors presented beautifully woven and embroidered pieces to neighboring countries. Women in ancient China developed the silk industry. They began making silk cloth in Stone Age (Neolithic) times, but the rest of the world did not discover their production secrets until many centuries later. Han traders, who carried the precious fabric along the Silk Road to the west, sold a roll of silk for the same price as 795 lb (360 kg) of rice. In Rome, the writer Pliny complained that women's desire to wear silk was ruining the Roman Empire.

EMBROIDERED SILK
In this piece, colored silk and gold-covered threads delicately pattern a cream background. Flower and bird designs were much loved from Tang times onward.

STRANGE BUT TRUE
Silk was very precious. Pliny thought silk came from "the hair of the sea-sheep." Silkworms raised for their thread today eat only mulberry leaves and must be protected from noise, vibrations and strong smells.

PAINTING ON SILK
This painting of four scholars was done on the finest silk, which provided a smooth surface to paint on. But first it had to be coated with a substance called alum to prevent the inks from soaking into the fabric.

WEAVING SILK

The finest quality silk had six or seven smooth filaments twisted to form the thread. Coarser weaves had more. The weavers (shown below) fastened the ends of the vertical warp threads to belts around their waists and held them tight with bars under their feet. They were then able to pass the horizontal weft threads over and under the warp threads.

SILK PRODUCTION

The ancient Chinese gathered mulberry leaves to feed the caterpillars they raised to spin their silky coverings. Women rinsed the cocoons in hot water to loosen the filaments of thread before the adult moths could bite their way out.

Discover more in Clothing and Jewelry

Arched bridge
Engineer Li Chun designed an arched bridge in AD 610. It was stronger and took less stone to build than other bridges.

Horsepower
The Han invented trace (or breast) harnesses for horses. These replaced choking throat straps and greatly increased the animals' pulling power.

• DISCOVERY, ART AND INVENTION •

New Ideas

The ancient Chinese were always looking for practical ways to solve problems. Farmers hung bags of killer ants in their orchards to eat the insect pests that would otherwise have destroyed the mandarin orange crop. Ancient Chinese inventors were way ahead of the rest of the world. They developed wheelbarrows, for example, about 1,300 years before Europeans copied the idea. Their inventions of paper, printing, the compass and gunpowder have probably had more impact on the world than anything else that has ever been invented. The earliest compass, called a "south-pointing fish," consisted of a wooden fish containing a piece of metal floating in a bowl of water. Gunpowder, made from saltpeter, sulfur and charcoal, was used by alchemists and physicians long before it was used for weapons. Other notable inventions included matches, the game of chess and mechanical clocks.

Rudder
Ancient Chinese ships had rudders, essential for steering properly, by the first century AD. European navigators began to use rudders around AD 1180.

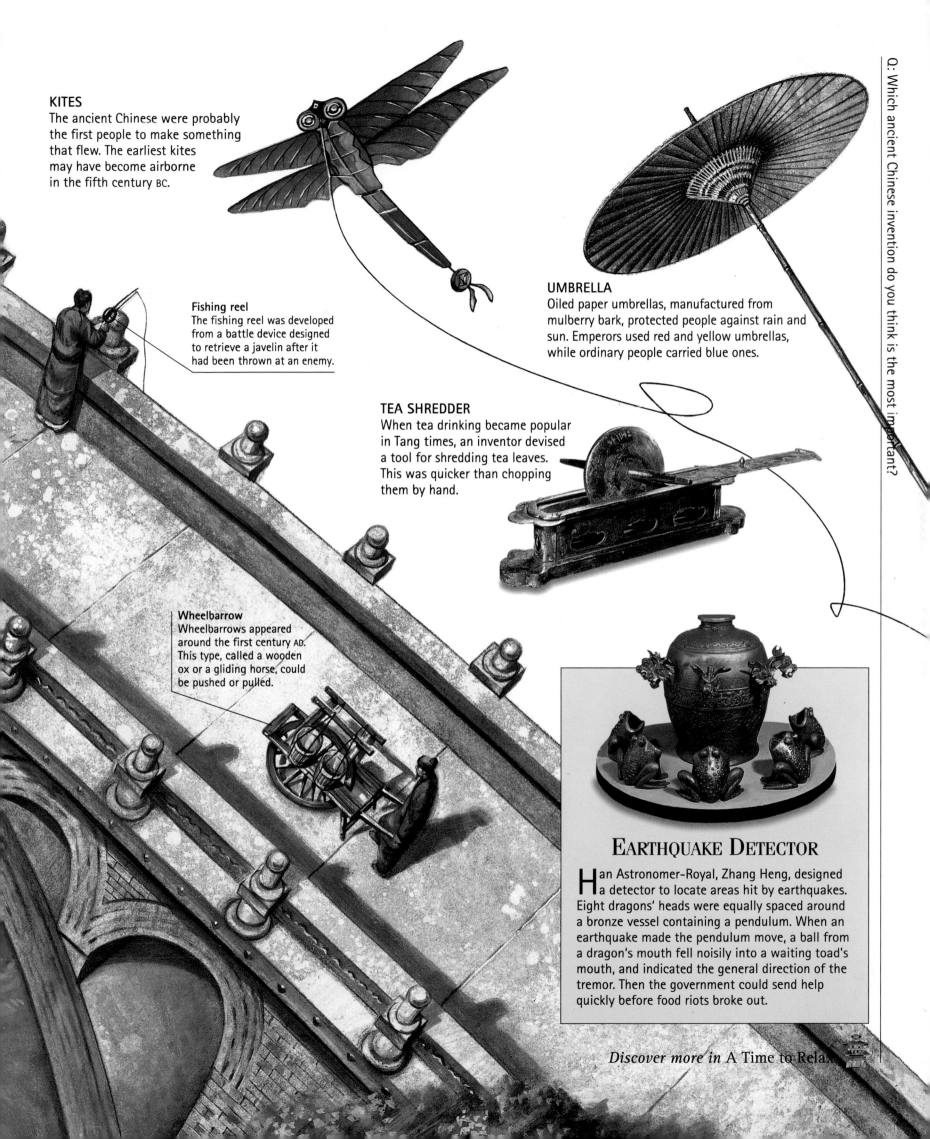

KITES
The ancient Chinese were probably the first people to make something that flew. The earliest kites may have become airborne in the fifth century BC.

Fishing reel
The fishing reel was developed from a battle device designed to retrieve a javelin after it had been thrown at an enemy.

UMBRELLA
Oiled paper umbrellas, manufactured from mulberry bark, protected people against rain and sun. Emperors used red and yellow umbrellas, while ordinary people carried blue ones.

TEA SHREDDER
When tea drinking became popular in Tang times, an inventor devised a tool for shredding tea leaves. This was quicker than chopping them by hand.

Wheelbarrow
Wheelbarrows appeared around the first century AD. This type, called a wooden ox or a gliding horse, could be pushed or pulled.

EARTHQUAKE DETECTOR

Han Astronomer-Royal, Zhang Heng, designed a detector to locate areas hit by earthquakes. Eight dragons' heads were equally spaced around a bronze vessel containing a pendulum. When an earthquake made the pendulum move, a ball from a dragon's mouth fell noisily into a waiting toad's mouth, and indicated the general direction of the tremor. Then the government could send help quickly before food riots broke out.

Discover more in A Time to Relax

When the Mongols conquered China and founded the Yuan dynasty, they brought great wealth to the country through international trade. Kublai Khan was the most famous Mongolian emperor.

SONG DYNASTY (960–1279)
The Song expanded foreign trade and built sea-going junks with sails. Navigators consulted star charts and adapted the "south-pointing fish" compass for use at sea.

SEATED IN PEACE
Yuan sculptors introduced a more elegant figure style. This bronze statue of Bodhisattva Guanyin, made in 1339, was a Buddhists monk's offering in his search for enlightenment.

DRAGON POWER
Dragons continued to be a popular theme in Song art. This jade plaque, depicting two of the mythical creatures intertwined, shows how advanced jade work had become.

• DISCOVERY, ART AND INVENTION •

Into the Modern World

When we refer to ancient China, we are describing a period of time, rather than the rise and fall of a civilization. Ancient China did not disappear like ancient Egypt or the Roman Empire. Imperial Chinese rule survived until the twentieth century. When the Tang fell from power in AD 906, north and south China were briefly divided during the period of the Five Dynasties and Ten Kingdoms. The Song dynasty reunited the country. Invaders from Mongolia set up the Yuan dynasty, only to be driven out by the Ming after less than 100 years. In 1644, conquering tribes from northern Manchu established China's final dynasty—the Qing. Each dynasty used achievements from the past but also developed in its own way. New styles of art and craft, for example, flourished in the Ming era, but Qin Shi Huangdi's system of writing changed little until present times.

MING DYNASTY (1368–1644)
Ming emperors were constantly threatened by the Mongols, who fought to regain their lost empire. The Ming rebuilt the Qin dynasty's Long Wall into the Great Wall of China.

QING DYNASTY (1644–1912)
China's empire grew weaker toward the end of the Qing dynasty. In 1908, three-year-old Puyi became the last emperor. He was forced to abdicate (give up his throne) on February 12, 1912.

CHINA FROM CHINA
In the eighteenth century, scenes of the waterfront in Canton, such as this one on a Qing porcelain punchbowl, were painted for European traders to take home as souvenirs.

PRICELESS VASE
The Ming dynasty is famous for ceramics. Ming blue-and-white porcelain dishes, bowls and containers of all types became prized throughout the world.

STRANGE BUT TRUE
The last emperor was treated like a living god until he was six. He became a gardener and citizen of the People's Republic of China and died at the age of sixty-two.

THE PEOPLE'S REPUBLIC OF CHINA

The republic that replaced imperial government in China was threatened by Japanese invasion in 1937. It joined briefly with the communist party to fight against the Japanese. Unsettled times in China ended when the communist party, led by Mao Zedong (above left), gained power in 1949. Mao ruled China until his death in September 1976.

Discover more in Order in Society

Discovering Ancient China

When people die, the objects they leave behind tell us much about how they lived. Such evidence becomes more difficult to find as time goes on because all materials do not last well. As centuries slip by, natural disasters such as floods and earthquakes destroy villages, towns and even cities. Abandoned settlements often become buried and forgotten. We are fortunate that the early Chinese made things of bronze, clay and jade, and wrote on bone and shell. We are lucky, too, that they placed their dead in sealed underground tombs with treasure stores of beautiful artwork and household possessions. Their passion for keeping detailed records of government affairs also helps us to find out about dynasties from long ago. Discovering ancient China is an ongoing process and thousands of sites across the country are still being examined. Little by little, archaeologists are digging up China's past.

RICE FARMING TODAY
In the paddy fields of present-day China, the farmers go about their work in much the same way as they did in ancient times.

CHARIOTS OF BRONZE
Archaeologists document every find with absolute precision. These chariots unearthed in a chamber on the western side of the First Emperor's tomb in 1980 have been restored to near-perfect condition.

REMARKABLE REMAINS
Lady Xin, Marquise of Dai died sometime after 168 BC. X-rays of her well-preserved remains found the cause of death was a heart attack. She had just eaten a large piece of melon and 138 seeds were discovered inside her.

PRESERVED ON PAPER

The dry atmosphere in the Buddhist cave temples at Dunhuang on the edge of the desert preserved sculptures, silk paintings and paper pages, like this one.

ANCIENT VILLAGES

Banpo, near the modern city of Xi'an in northern China, was first settled at least 6,500 years ago. Archaeologists have learned much from excavating it and other Stone Age (Neolithic) sites. Houses had square, oblong or round frameworks of poles, plastered with mud and thatched with reeds. Potters produced well-shaped vessels without the help of a potter's wheel. They decorated them with bold designs and fired them in a kiln.

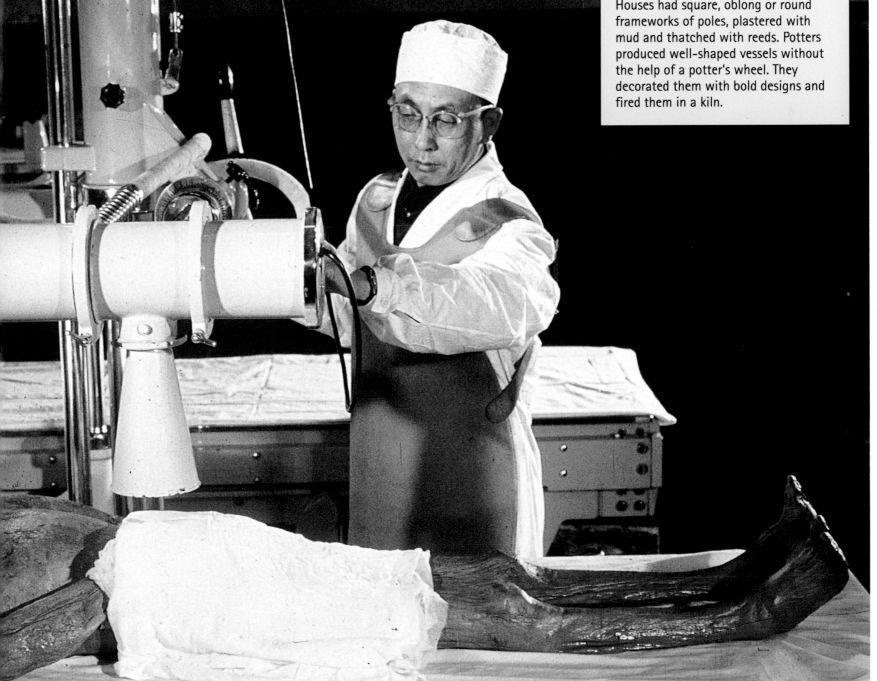

59

Dynasties of Ancient China

Many dynasties in ancient China lasted for hundreds of years. They took the family name of the first ruler. The emperor had more than one wife and there was usually an eldest son to take his place when he died. If there was no suitable son, another male heir was chosen from the family. It was very rare for a woman to hold power—Empress Wu Zetian was a notable exception. The most common way for a dynasty to end was when a strong opposing group seized government by force. The following list includes some of the most important rulers of ancient China. All dates before the Zhou dynasty are approximate.

Shang bronze

6000–1700 BC   **STONE AGE (NEOLITHIC) PERIOD**

Northeastern China
5000 BC	**Xinglongwa**
4500 BC	**Chahai**
4500–4000 BC	**Zhaobaogou**
3500–2500 BC	**Hongshan**

Stone Age (Neolithic) pottery

North central China
5000–3000 BC	**Central Yangshao**
3000–1500 BC	**Gansu Yangshao**

Eastern China
4500–2500 BC	**Dawenkou**
2500–1700 BC	**Longshan**

Southeastern China
5000–4500 BC	**Hemudu**
5000–4000 BC	**Majiabang**
4000–3000 BC	**Songze**
3000–2000 BC	**Liangzhu**

South central China
4000–3300 BC	**Daxi**
2500–2000 BC	**Shijiahe**

South China
3000–2000 BC	**Shixia**

2000–1600 BC	**ERLITOU PERIOD**

1600–1050 BC   **SHANG DYNASTY**
1600–1400 BC Erligang period
1400–1050 BC Anyang period

1050–771 BC   **WESTERN ZHOU DYNASTY**

770–221 BC   **EASTERN ZHOU DYNASTY**
770–475 BC   Spring and Autumn period
475–221 BC   Warring States period

221–207 BC   **QIN DYNASTY**
221–210 BC   Qin Shi Huangdi reigns
209–206 BC   Second emperor of Qin reigns

Zhou bronze

206 BC–AD 9	**WESTERN HAN DYNASTY**	
	202–195 BC	Gaodi reigns
	141–87 BC	Wudi reigns

| AD 9–25 | **XIN DYNASTY** | |

Han pottery

AD 25–220	**EASTERN HAN DYNASTY**	
	AD 25–57	Guangwudi reigns
	AD 58–75	Mingdi reigns
	AD 88–105	Hedi reigns

AD 221–280	**THREE KINGDOMS**	
	220–265	Wei
	221–263	Shu
	222–280	Wu

Qin terra cotta

AD 420–589	**SOUTHERN DYNASTIES**	
	420–479	Liu Song
	479–502	Southern Qi
	502–557	Liang
	557–589	Chen

| AD 581–618 | **SUI DYNASTY** | |

AD 618–906	**TANG DYNASTY**	
	618–626	Gaozu reigns
	626–649	Taizong reigns
	649–683	Gaozong reigns
	690–705	Empress Wu Zetian reigns
	712–756	Xuanzong reigns
	888–904	Zhaozong reigns
	904–907	Aizong reigns

| AD 265–316 | **WESTERN JIN DYNASTY** | |

| AD 317–420 | **EASTERN JIN DYNASTY** | |

AD 386–581	**NORTHERN DYNASTIES**	
	386–535	Northern Wei
	534–550	Eastern Wei
	535–557	Western Wei
	550–577	Northern Qi
	557–581	Northern Zhou

Tang pottery

Glossary

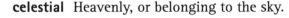

Shang bronze statue

abrasive A material with a rough texture used for smoothing. The ancient Chinese worked jade by rubbing it with sand.

acupuncture A Chinese treatment for illness, first practiced in ancient times. It involves inserting needles under the skin at certain points on the body.

AD An abbreviation for the Latin *anno Domini*, meaning "in the year of our Lord." Used for the measurement of time, AD indicates the number of years since the estimated date of Christ's birth.

alchemist A person who seeks to change base metals into gold and searches for the elixir of life. Alchemists in ancient China practiced part magic and part chemistry.

anonymous Without a name. The work of individual artisans in ancient China was not acknowledged by name.

archaeologist A person who studies the way people in the past lived by analyzing the things they left behind, such as tomb goods, tools, weapons and cooking pots.

bamboo A treelike grass with a hollow, woody stem. The ancient Chinese wrote on long strips of bamboo.

barbarians The ancient Chinese name for the people who lived beyond China's borders and did not share its customs.

BC Before Christ. Used for the measurement of time, BC indicates the number of years before the estimated date of Christ's birth.

bi disk A round shape, made of jade or some other material.

Beacon tower ruins from the Long Wall

bronze An alloy (mixture) of copper and tin and sometimes lead.

calligraphy The art of writing with a brush dipped in ink. Faultless writing looked natural and "alive" with strong strokes, invisible joins and even-textured ink.

camphor A sharp-smelling substance taken from camphor trees. The ancient Chinese used it to flavor sweet dishes. Today it is often used as an ingredient in mothballs, ointments for injured joints and to treat colds.

Terra-cotta granary

canal An artificial waterway. Canals in ancient China were dug by hand.

Zhou jade disks

celestial Heavenly, or belonging to the sky.

ceramics Articles produced from clay and other substances that have been fired in a kiln.

charcoal The carbon remains of burned materials. It was used as an ingredient in gunpowder.

Chinese parsley (coriander) An herb used by the ancient Chinese for medicinal purposes. It was eaten to relieve indigestion and made into a lotion to bathe patients with measles.

civilization An organized society that has developed social customs, government, technology and the arts.

cocoon The protective covering woven by certain insects, such as moths and butterflies, when they are in the chrysalis stage of growing from grubs or caterpillars into the adult stage of their life cycle.

dragon A mythical creature. The ancient Chinese worshipped the spirits of dragons. The five-toed dragon became the First Emperor's special symbol. Dragons were thought to control thunderstorms and rainfall.

dyke A barrier to stop water from flooding. The ancient Chinese tried to control a flooding river by building a dyke. They drove stakes into the banks and piled bundles of sticks against them.

dynasty A ruling family. Members of a dynasty were related by birth, marriage or adoption.

elixir A magical mixture that is supposed to enable people to live forever.

Ferghana horses Horses imported from central Asia. The ancient Chinese could not breed horses easily themselves.

fodder The feed grown for livestock.

garlic An herb used by the ancient Chinese to treat colds, whooping cough and other illnesses.

garnet A semi-precious stone that is glassy red, yellow or green.

ginseng An herb used by the ancient Chinese for medicinal purposes. It was prescribed for poor appetites, some forms of upset stomachs and coughs, excessive perspiring and forgetfulness.

glaze A shiny coating that gives a smooth, glossy surface. Glaze is usually applied to pottery or porcelain, but other materials can also be glazed.

hemp A plant with tough fibers that can be woven into fabric and rope.

inlay A form of decoration in which one material is inserted into prepared slots or cavities in the surface of another material to form a pattern or a picture. The ancient Chinese often inlaid bronze with silver.

irrigation The process of supplying water to the land using canals or ditches.

jade An extremely hard mineral. The jade in ancient China was nephrite, a white stone streaked with reds or browns. The more familiar green jadeite was not known in China until much later.

junk A Chinese sailing boat. Chinese boat builders stiffened the sails with bamboo rods.

Kashgar A country in ancient Asia.

lacquer A natural plastic varnish that resists heat, moisture, acids, alkalis and bacteria, and is made from the milky sap of the lacquer tree. The ancient Chinese heated and purified this substance and then painted many very thin coats onto objects made from bamboo, silk, wood and other materials.

li A Chinese unit of length. One li equals about $^3/_{10}$ mile (0.5 km).

linear Made up of lines. The linear designs on Stone Age (Neolithic) pottery were made with a soft brush.

magistrate A government official who judged the local criminals and looked after the affairs of a district or province.

minister A high-ranking government official who advised the emperor and helped to see that imperial laws were obeyed.

moxibustion An ancient Chinese treatment to relieve pain. Small amounts of dried moxa leaves (mugwort) were burned and applied to certain parts of the body.

Neolithic A period of time when humans made tools and weapons of flint and stone. Neolithic is the final stage of the Stone Age.

nomads People who move continually from place to place to find food for themselves and pasture for their animals. They do not settle in permanent homes.

plaque A wall ornament in the form of a plate or tile, made from porcelain, wood or other material.

porcelain A thin china made from fine kaolin clay that was found in the Chinese mountains.

production line The process of working in a team to produce something. The tasks are divided up so that workers become very fast and good at what they do, for example, gilding the handles of a lacquer cup.

pupate The process in the life cycle of certain insects when the creature changes from a grub or a caterpillar into the adult stage of development.

qilin A mythical animal also called a Chinese unicorn. It symbolized long life, greatness, happiness and wise government.

republic A form of government in which the people elect representatives.

ritual A set pattern of behavior for a religious or other kind of ceremony.

rudder A flat piece of wood attached to the stern of a boat below the waterline, which is used for steering. The rudder was a Chinese invention.

saltpeter (potassium nitrate) A chemical ingredient of gunpowder.

star anise An herb used as a medicine by the ancient Chinese, for example, to relieve stomach pain and vomiting.

Stone Age The time when humans made tools and weapons from stone.

sulfur A chemical ingredient of gunpowder.

terra cotta A hard, unglazed, reddish-brown clay. The ancient Chinese made terra-cotta models and figures to be placed in tombs.

warp The threads arranged vertically on a weaving loom. The weft threads are woven through the warp threads.

weft The threads woven across the fabric (horizontally) on a weaving loom.

Xiongnu Nomadic people who lived to the north of China.

zither A stringed instrument. The seven-stringed zither was one of the oldest instruments in ancient China.

Bronze and turquoise bird

Han bronze seal

Tang pottery dancer

Tang pottery camel

Index

Picture Credits

(t=top, b=bottom, l=left, r=right, c=center, i=icon, F=front, C=cover, B=back, Bg=background)
Ancient Art & Architecture Collection, 14cl, 62cl (B. Crisp). Asian Art and Archaeology, 7cr, 9r, 9tr, 15c, 19tl, 23cr, 24bl, 24t, 38bc, 38bl, 55cr, 60tr, 62tl. Asian Art Museum of San Francisco, 32tc, 62bcl (B60 P130+, The Avery Brundage Collection). The British Library, 47cr (S. 3326), 48tl (Or 8210/P2). The British Museum, 3, 5br, 7tcr, 10tl, 15br, 28bl, 29r, 35tr, 35tl, 45tc, 50bl, 51br, 51tcr, 51tr, 52cl, 56cl, 57cl, 59tl, 59tr, 62bl. Cambridge University Library, 13br (By permission of the Syndics). China Pictorial, 22t, 26tl, 27br, 34cl, 36bc, 38c, 38tl, 47t, 58/59b, 60l. China Stock, 23br, 43cr. The Commercial Press (Hong Kong) Ltd, 45tl (From Chinese Textile Designs). Cultural Relics Publishing House, 4b, 8bl, 15cr, 16cl, 21tr, 22bl, 26tc, 37bl, 41br, 46bl, 48tr, 63tcr, 63tr. Giraudon, 40cl, 57br, 63cr (Bonora/Musee Guimet, Paris), 51cr, 53c, 60br (Lauros), 35tl, 61tr (Lauros/Musee de la Ville de Paris, Musee Cernuschi), 50cl, 56bl (Lauros/Musee Guimet, Paris). The Image Bank, 57bc (P. & G. Bowater). Institute of History and Philology, Academia Sinica, Taipei, 9tc. Cecilia Lindqvist, Stockholm, 32tr, 32tl.

Mary Evans Picture Library, 23tr. Museum of Far Eastern Antiquities, Stockholm, Sweden, 7tr (E. Cornelius). National Museums of Scotland, 43br. The Nelson-Atkins Museum of Art, Kansas City, Missouri, 10bl (Purchase: Nelson Trust, 33-81), 20bl (Purchase: Nelson Trust, 49-40), 34tl (Purchase: Nelson Trust, 35-125/1), 45tr, 63br (Gift of Earle Grant, 59-63). New World Press, Beijing, 58bl. The Palace Museum, Beijing, 52bl. The Photo Library, Sydney, 15tr (Hulton-Deutsch). Robert Harding Picture Library, 18tr, 19tc, 58tr (G. Corrigan). Royal Ontario Museum, 41cr. Scala, 7br (Giuganno Collection, Rome). Daniel Schwartz, Zurich, 16b, 16c, 17c, 61l. The Science Museum, London, 55br (Science & Society Picture Library). The Seattle Art Museum, 44tr (P. Macapia/Eugene Fuller Memorial Collection). Werner Forman Archive, 12tl, 26bl, 37c, 37cl, 47br (Eskenazi Ltd, London), 24br (Myron Falk, New York), 20cl (Idemitsu Museum of Arts, Tokyo), 48cr (Brian McElney Collection, Hong Kong), 50c (Earl Morse, New York), 40bl (National Palace Museum, Taipei), 41tr, 48tcr (Private Collection, New York), 20tl (Rene Rivkin, Sydney), 41tr (Sotheby's, London), 30bc (Victoria & Albert Museum, London).

Illustration Credits

Paul Bachem, 24/25c. Andrew Beckett/Garden Studio, 52/53c, 52tl, 53br. Leslye Cole/Alex Lavroff & Associates, 28/29c. Chris Forsey, 18/19b, 19tr. John Crawford Fraser, 56/57t. Lorraine Hannay, 16tl, 17tr, 48/49b, 48l, 49r, 50/51c. Richard Hook/Bernard Thornton Artists, UK, 38/39c, 39bc. Janet Jones/Alex Lavroff & Associates, 8/9c, 30/31c, 30l, 34/35c. Robyn Latimer, 29tr. Shane Marsh/Linden Artists Ltd, 32/33c, 33tl. Iain McKellar, 6/7c. Peter Mennim, 1, 4l, 36l, 36r, 37r. Darren Pattenden/Garden Studio, 26/27c. Tony Pyrzakowski, 2, 22/23c, 40/41c, 44/45b. John Richards, 11–14c. Trevor Ruth, 46/47c. Mark Sofilas/Alex Lavroff & Associates, 5tr, 54/55c. Sharif Tarabay/Garden Studio, 42/43c. C. Winston Taylor, 10/15c, 20/21c. Rod Westblade, endpapers, icons. David Wun, 49tl.

Cover Credits

Asian Art and Archaeology, BC. China Pictorial, FCtr. China Stock, Bg. Lorraine Hannay, FCtl. John Richards, FCc.